M000014365

ESPECIALLY FOR

_____

FROM

_____

DATE

_____

*To my dogs, whose paw prints are all over this book,
and in memory of our very special Alexis Grace.*

© 2010 by Barbour Publishing, Inc.

Written and compiled by Pamela McQuade.

ISBN 978-1-60260-821-4

All rights reserved. No part of this publication may be reproduced or transmitted for commercial purposes, except for brief quotations in printed reviews, without written permission of the publisher.

Scripture quotations, unless otherwise indicated, are taken from the HOLY BIBLE, NEW INTERNATIONAL VERSION®. NIV®. Copyright © 1973, 1978, 1984 by International Bible Society. Used by permission of Zondervan. All rights reserved.

Scripture quotations marked ESV are from The Holy Bible, English Standard Version®, copyright © 2001 by Crossway Bibles, a publishing ministry of Good News Publishers. Used by permission. All rights reserved.

Scripture quotations marked NASB are taken from the New American Standard Bible, © 1960, 1962, 1963, 1968, 1971, 1972, 1973, 1975, 1977, 1995 by The Lockman Foundation. Used by permission.

Scripture quotations marked KJV are taken from the King James Version of the Bible.

Scripture quotations marked NKJV are taken from the New King James Version®. Copyright © 1982 by Thomas Nelson, Inc. Used by permission. All rights reserved.

Published by Barbour Publishing, Inc., P.O. Box 719, Uhrichsville, Ohio 44683, www.barbourbooks.com

Our mission is to publish and distribute inspirational products offering exceptional value and biblical encouragement to the masses.

 Member of the
Evangelical Christian
Publishers Association

Printed in China.

Thank Heaven for

DOGS

· and other little pleasures ·

BARBOUR
PUBLISHING

UNSELFISH FRIEND

The one absolute, unselfish friend that a man can have in this selfish world—the one that never deserts him, the one that never proves ungrateful or treacherous—is his dog.

GEORGE GRAHAM VEST

DOG COUNT

If you think dogs can't count, try putting three dog biscuits in your pocket and then giving Fido only two of them.

PHIL PASTORET

MY DOG AND I

When living seems but little worth
And all things go awry,
I close the door, we journey forth—
My dog and I! . . .

And ere we reach the busy town,
Like birds my troubles fly,
We are two comrades glad of heart—
My dog and I!

ALICE J. CLEATOR

A COMMON GIFT

The dog is the most faithful of animals and would be much esteemed were it not so common. Our Lord God has made His greatest gift the commonest.

MARTIN LUTHER

DOGS AND CHILDREN

Youngsters of the age of two and three are endowed with extraordinary strength. They can lift a dog twice their own weight and dump him into the bathtub.

ERMA BOMBECK

INTERSPECIES FUN

The dog has got more fun out of Man than Man
has got out of the dog, for the clearly demonstrable
reason that Man is the more laughable of the two
animals.

JAMES THURBER

GEM?

Mother is going to present Gem to
Uncle Will. . . . Gem is really a very nice
small bow-wow, but Mother found that in this
case possession was less attractive than pursuit.
When she takes him out walking, he carries her
along as if she were a Roman chariot.

THEODORE ROOSEVELT

MY DOG'S NEEDS

Lord, I know You value this dog whom You've created. May every moment of care I give to my dog reflect Your love for Your creation, and may it bring joy to me and my dog.

FAITH AND PET CARE

I care not much for a man's religion whose dog and cat are not the better for it.

ABRAHAM LINCOLN

CHOSEN

A shelter dog looks at your face, wags her back end, and gives you that adoring, "take me home, please" look. Your heart melts, and something clicks. "This is the one," you declare, and you think you've selected a wonderful dog.

Not really; *she's* chosen *you*!

GOOD HOME

A house without either a cat or a
dog is the house of a scoundrel.

PORTUGUESE PROVERB

CRUMBS

Then she came and worshiped Him, saying, "Lord, help me!" But He answered and said, "It is not good to take the children's bread and throw *it* to the little dogs." And she said, "Yes, Lord, yet even the little dogs eat the crumbs which fall from their masters' table."

MATTHEW 15:25–27 NKJV

HEART SIZE

When they come to live with us, dogs never look at the size of our homes. They only judge us by the size of our hearts.

ETERNAL HAPPINESS

God will prepare everything for our perfect happiness in heaven, and if it takes my dog being there, I believe he'll be there.

BILLY GRAHAM

BEST FRIENDS

Thank You, Lord, for the joys of having a dog.
Help me to find enough time to play with him,
walk him, and care for him. May he not only
be my best friend, may I be his.

NOBLE COMPANION

Recollect that the Almighty, who gave the dog to be companion of our pleasures and our toils, hath invested him with a nature noble and incapable of deceit.

SIR WALTER SCOTT

SPOILED?

Now it seems that every dog not only must have its day, it also has its bed (yours), its couch (ditto), and a personal groomer, too.

DOGGY DOOR

A door is what a dog is perpetually on the wrong side of.

OGDEN NASH

EAGER LEARNER

Think of your dog as a sponge, willing to take everything in and eager to learn new things. . . . A dog is a living creature with a hungry mind and a great capacity for love and gratitude—as long as you keep her interested and excited about life.

TAMAR GELLER

KNOWING A DOG

After years of having a dog, you know him.
You know the meaning of his snuffs and grunts
and barks. Every twitch of the ears is a question or
statement, every wag of the tail is an exclamation.

ROBERT R. MCCAMMON

TWO SPECIES

*Lord, You have placed this helpless puppy in my arms.
As two very different species, we're likely to have
communication gaps. Please help me appreciate my dog,
and nurture growth and understanding between us.*

TAIL-WAGGING JOY

In times of joy, all of us wished we possessed a tail we could wag.

W. H. AUDEN

INTERSPECIES RELATIONSHIPS

The best training for dog–cat relationships is
a cat with very sharp claws and the will to swat
once or twice at the dog's nose. Any dog with
sense quickly gets the message and gains an
unending respect for every cat it meets.

LONELY LIVING

Living on your own is lonely. Eventually, you may start thinking about a dog. . . . But can you care for the needs of a dog?. . . Before you adopt that puppy, be sure you are ready for a fifteen-year commitment.

TONI SORTOR

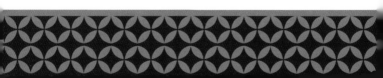

DANGEROUS OCCUPATION

Like one who seizes a dog by the ears is a passer-by
who meddles in a quarrel not his own.

PROVERBS 26:17

FOLLOW WITH DETERMINATION

The scent hound is a model of perseverance, Lord.
He holds to a trail without deviation, all the way to the
end. May I follow as determinedly after You as that
hound pursues the track of some small creature.

CONSCIENCE GUIDE

If a dog will not come to you after having looked you in the face, you should go home and examine your conscience.

WOODROW WILSON

AN OLDER DOG'S LIFE

Sleep till you're hungry; eat till you're sleepy.

ANONYMOUS

DOGGY DISTINCTION

[Following Egypt's final plague] "There will be loud wailing throughout Egypt—worse than there has ever been or ever will be again. But among the Israelites not a dog will bark at any man or animal." Then you will know that the LORD makes a distinction between Egypt and Israel.

EXODUS 11:6–7

TRAINING CHALLENGE

I can train any dog in five minutes. It's training the owner that takes longer.

BARBARA WOODHOUSE

GUILTY!

Your dog, who has just snatched the last slices
of your loaf of bread, looks up with such
appealing eyes. You know she's sorry—
until she grabs the peanut butter jar, too.

DRIVING WITH DOGS

The pattern was always the same, Dan stretched on the passenger seat with his head on my knee, Hector peering through the windshield, his paws balanced on my hand as it rested on the gear lever. . . . Hector hated to miss a thing.

JAMES HERRIOT

SECURITY HOUNDS

Though they may seem totally carefree and happy-go-lucky, puppies actually need a deep sense of security in their lives. Keeping them on a regular schedule will help them develop into emotionally well-rounded dogs.

THE DOG'S HOUSE

Home, the spot of earth supremely blest,
A dearer, sweeter spot than all the rest.

ROBERT MONTGOMERY

RESURRECTION DAY

Be thou comforted, little dog, thou too in
Resurrection shall have a little golden tail.

MARTIN LUTHER

DOG WORDS

It's easy to see dogs are popular in English-speaking nations by looking at this sampling of words or expressions that relate to them: top dog, legal beagle, dog in the manger, shaggy-dog story, dog paddle, dog and pony show, dogged, dog-ear, dogface, hot dog, dog days, sea dog. . .

HONESTY

Although the dispositions of dogs are as various as their forms. . .to the credit of their name be it said, a dog never sullies his mouth with an untruth.

ALFRED ELWES

A DOG'S LOVE

For love, that comes wherever life and sense
Are given by God, in thee was most intense;
A chain of heart, a feeling of the mind,
A tender sympathy, which did thee bind
Not only to us Men, but to thy Kind.

WILLIAM WORDSWORTH

DOG'S JUDGMENT

The censure of a dog is something
no man can stand.

CHRISTOPHER MORLEY

HEARTWARMING

Foster dogs for a shelter or rescue, and you'll leave pieces of your heart spread across the land. But the sweet memories of wonderful dogs and their compassionate humans form a warm quilt against the cold loss of their presence.

FIDO OF THE FUTURE

The factory of the future will have only two employees, a man and a dog. The man will be there to feed the dog. The dog will be there to keep the man from touching the equipment.

WARREN G. BENNIS

MY BEST FRIEND

If I was sad, then he had grief, as well—
Seeking my hands with soft insistent paw,
Searching my face with anxious eyes that saw
More than my halting, human speech could tell;
Eyes wide with wisdom, fine, compassionate—
Dear, loyal one, that knew not wrong nor hate.

MERIBAH ABBOTT

DOG TRAINING IN LOVE

Love is patient, love is kind. . .it is not proud.
It is not self-seeking, it is not easily angered,
it keeps no record of wrongs. It always protects,
always trusts, always hopes, always perseveres.

1 Corinthians 13:4–5, 7

FUTURE VIEW

As you're raising your puppy, keep an eye on what you want her to be in the future. Behaviors such as nipping or barking, which seem cute in a puppy, could be disastrous in an adult dog.

LADDIE'S ANSWER

Nay, brother of the sod
What part hast thou in God?
What spirit art thou of?
It answers, "Love."

KATHARINE LEE BATES

HOUND'S ADMONITION
TO HUMANS

There is not a time that you walk through the street,
when if you employed your senses, you would not
learn something worthwhile.

HENRY WARD BEECHER

JOYFUL LOVE

Love animals: God has given them the
rudiments of thought and joy untroubled.
Do not trouble their joy, don't harass them,
don't deprive them of their happiness,
don't work against God's intent.

FYODOR DOSTOYEVSKY

BONDING

People bond with their dogs by creating a happy environment. . . . The key to being a successful dog owner is your emotional relationship with the animal.

MORDECAI SIEGAL AND MATTHEW MARGOLIS

DOGFIGHT

It's not the size of the dog in the fight, it's the size of the fight in the dog.

MARK TWAIN

DAY OFF

Need a vacation, but don't have time? Take your dog to a park, beach, or on a hike. No one enjoys fun as much as your four-legged friend. In an hour or so, he'll have you frolicking, too, if you let him show the way.

THE JOY OF A DOG

The great pleasure of a dog is that you
may make a fool of yourself with him and
not only will he not scold you, but he
will make a fool of himself, too.

SAMUEL BUTLER

LAPDOG

I am a much better person with a dog in my lap.

JOHN O'HURLEY

A DOG'S LOVE PERSPECTIVE

Give, and it will be given to you. A good measure, pressed down, shaken together and running over.

LUKE 6:38

CANINE VISION

Help me, Lord, to sometimes see life through my dog's eyes. May I appreciate the joy of greeting someone I love and delight in the cool morning breeze as we take a long walk together.

MY DOG DASH

I have a dog of Blenheim birth,
With fine long ears and full of mirth;
And sometimes, running o'er the plain,
He tumbles on his nose:
But quickly jumping up again,
Like lightning on he goes!

JOHN RUSKIN

SENSITIVE SCHNOZ

Smell is supremely important to dogs. . . . The average dog's nose is about 10,000 to 100,000 times more sensitive than our own.

DAVID TAYLOR

APPRECIATING GIFTS

Some humans love terriers, others retrievers; some adore sheepdogs, while others cotton up to hounds. Like dogs, people are all different, but there's a breed for any one of us.

INTELLIGENT SHEEPDOG

This honest sheepdog's countenance I read;
With him can talk; nor blush to waste a word
On creatures less intelligent and shrewd.

WILLIAM WORDSWORTH

A GENTLE HAND

The impact of gentle handling can be seen even if it occurs before birth: puppies born to mothers who were petted during pregnancy tend to be more receptive to handling after birth.

PATRICIA B. MCCONNELL

FAVORITE CHEW

No matter how many toys, bones, and treats you buy, your puppy's favorite chew is still likely to be that sock you've only worn twice or your most treasured pair of shoes.

A DOG'S BEDTIME PRAYER

I will lie down and sleep in peace, for you alone,
O LORD, make me dwell in safety.

PSALM 4:8

SMART PUP!

Extremely smart dogs are typically very challenging pets because they learn not just what you want them to learn, but all sorts of other things as well. They are very observant. . .which is why they sometimes seem to read our minds.

KIM SAUNDERS

HOWLSPEAK

Dogs howl to "talk" to other members
of the pack. Generally speaking, a howl
says "Where are you?" If your dog howls
when left alone, it is bored.

BRUCE FOGLE

CONGRESSIONAL POOCH

My dog can bark like a congressman, fetch like an aide, beg like a press secretary, and play dead like a receptionist when the phone rings.

U.S. CONGRESSMAN GERALD B. H. SOLOMON

MAX-ED OUT?

According to a pet-tag company, the most common name for a male dog in the United States, Australia, and New Zealand is Max. Maggie was the favorite female name in the United States, and Jessie topped the charts in Australia.

WILLING SHEEPDOG

A dog will look at you as if to say, "What do you want me to do for you? I'll do anything for you." Whether a dog can in fact, do anything for you if you don't have sheep (I never have) is another matter. The dog is willing.

ROY BLOUNT JR.

WONDROUS DESIGN

Lord, You've helped me appreciate how wondrously You've made the dog. Out of all the animals You made, this one was designed as my special companion and friend. Thank You.

TAIL-WAGGER

The reason dogs have so many friends is because they wag their tails instead of their tongues.

ANONYMOUS

INFLUENCE LIMITATIONS

If you get to thinking you're a person of some influence, try ordering somebody else's dog around.

WILL ROGERS

PERSUASION

Nobody ever saw a dog make a fair and deliberate exchange of one bone for another with another dog. . . . When an animal wants to obtain something. . .it has no other means of persuasion but to gain the favor of those whose services it requires.

ADAM SMITH

POWER STRUGGLE

Isn't it amazing how powerful a dog becomes
as soon as it stretches out on the human's bed?
A fifty-pound, dead-weight dog can take up more
space than the average woman. He'll also make
her apologize for wanting more than a quarter
of the bed for her own use.

NEW-DOG DECISION

The Master talked of buying a whalebone-and-steel-and-snow bull terrier, or a more formidable if more greedy Great Dane. But the Mistress wanted a collie. So they compromised by getting the collie.

ALBERT PAYSON TERHUNE

ATTRACTION

Humankind is drawn to dogs because they are so like ourselves—bumbling, affectionate, confused, easily disappointed, eager to be amused, grateful for kindness and the least attention.

PAM BROWN

HUNTING HOUNDS

My hounds are bred out of the Spartan kind,
So flew'd, so sanded, and their heads are hung
With ears that sweep away the morning dew;
Crook-knee'd, and dew-lapp'd like Thessalian bulls;
Slow in pursuit, but match'd in mouth like bells,
Each under each.

WILLIAM SHAKESPEARE

A CANINE'S HEART

A cheerful heart is good medicine.

PROVERBS 17:22

"JUST A DOG"

Lord, to many people I know this is "just a dog." But she is Your creation, designed with a sensitive nose, fast legs, and a wide-open heart. Thank You for this special gift You've given me. May she never be "just a dog" to me.

RULES OF THE HOUSE

All dogs are great opportunists. That's important to remember when you try to teach your puppy the rules of the house.

JOHN ROSS AND BARBARA MCKINNEY

RETRIEVER?

[Marley] was a master at pursuing his prey. It was the concept of returning it that he did not seem to quite grasp. His general attitude seemed to be, *If you want the stick back that bad, YOU jump in the water for it.*

JOHN GROGAN

RAINBOW COVENANT

"This is the sign of the covenant I am making between me and you and every living creature. . . . Whenever the rainbow appears in the clouds, I will see it and remember the everlasting covenant between God and all living creatures of every kind on the earth."

GENESIS 9:12, 16

WOOLF/DOG THOUGHT

One cannot think well, love well, sleep well, if one has not dined well.

VIRGINIA WOOLF

FEEDING FRENZY

Feed a dog twice a day, and when you sit down to lunch, large eyes will follow you. *How dare you not share?* they demand. *Don't you know how selfish that is?*

Give in, and you'll be feeding him diet dog food *and* seeing those eyes at breakfast and dinner, too.

CANINE WISDOM

A loving heart is the truest wisdom.

CHARLES DICKENS

MY BRINDLE BULL-TERRIER

My near little, queer little, dear little dog,
So fearless of man, yet afraid of a frog!
The nearest and queerest and dearest of all
The race that is loving and winning and small;
The sweetest, most faithful, the truest and best
Dispenser of merriment, love, and unrest!

COLETTA RYAN

LEARNING OPPORTUNITY

The time between one month and four months of age is an important socialization time in a puppy's life. Dogs learn more in these weeks than in the rest of their lives.

A NEWFOUNDLAND PUP

The dog proved rather a doubtful possession. . . .
Its appetite was tremendous, and its preference for
my society embarrassingly unrestrained. It would
not be content to sleep anywhere else than in my
room. . . . [But] part with him I could not; for Bob
loved me.

JACOB A. RIIS

DOG-CAT RELATIONS

Those who will play with cats must expect to be scratched.

MIGUEL DE CERVANTES

EAR ISSUE

Why do dachshunds wear their ears inside out?

P. G. WODEHOUSE

RIGHT SIZE?

To dogs, size doesn't matter. The smallest Chihuahua takes on a lumbering Labrador without a second thought—and he's likely to end up being the top dog, too!

CREATION DAY

And God said, "Let the land produce living creatures according to their kinds. . . ." God made the wild animals according to their kinds, the livestock according to their kinds, and all the creatures that move along the ground according to their kinds. And God saw that it was good.

GENESIS 1:24–25

VALUES CHECK

On a popular dog-intelligence-rating scale,
the bloodhound comes in well below the "smart"
rating. But ask any human if he'd rather have
the top-smarts-rated border collie scent out his
missing child, and he'd surely prefer that "stupid"
bloodhound's top-rated nose!

REAL CHARITY

A bone to the dog is not charity.
Charity is the bone shared with the dog,
when you are just as hungry as the dog.

JACK LONDON

MUTT PASSION

Do you love dogs passionately? Answer that the day you take your mutt to the dog park and come back knowing all the dogs' names but wondering, *What was the name of Butch's human?*

COUCH-POTATO CANINE

How beautiful it is to do nothing, and then rest afterward.

DANISH PROVERB

ALLERGY CHALLENGE

One learns to itch where one can scratch.

ERNEST BRAMAH

START THE CHORUS

One dog barks at something;
the rest bark at him.

CHINESE PROVERB

JIGSAW DOG

We met a foster dog, and something just clicked.
Instantaneously, he knew he was the right one
for us. We brought him home, and he fit into our
lives like a jigsaw-puzzle piece snapping into place.
Adopting him was the best unplanned plan in our
lives.

ANIMAL-SHELTER SIGN

CHILDREN LEFT UNATTENDED
WILL BE GIVEN A PUPPY OR KITTEN.

PUPPY PLAYTIME

Play is a puppy's delightful work. As she runs flat out, chasing a ball, leaps in the air to catch a Frisbee, or darts about after a beetle, she's engaged in the work of building strength.

HUMILIATION

I have been studying the traits and dispositions
of the "lower animals" (so called) and contrasting
them with the traits and dispositions of man.
I find the result humiliating to me.

MARK TWAIN

MORE THAN MILLIONS

Not Carnegie, Vanderbilt, and Astor together could have raised money enough to buy a quarter share in my little dog.

ERNEST THOMPSON SETON

HOME SWEET HOME

For an animal person, an animal-less home is no home at all.

CLEVELAND AMORY

JOYOUS REUNION

When his human comes in the door, a dog rushes up, wagging his tail in delight. Not even a spouse shows such joy after his beloved has been gone an hour.

DOG'S FUTURE

Therefore do not worry about tomorrow,
for tomorrow will worry about itself.
Each day has enough trouble of its own.

MATTHEW 6:34

SHORT DAYS

Thank You, Lord, for my lively little pup. Remind me that these days of puppyhood are short. Give me large doses of patience and love, along with enough determination to train her for a lifetime.

CHAIN-LINK DILEMMA

The grass is always greener on the other side of the fence.

PROVERB

CARB HOUNDS

The carb hounds of the dog world can grab a loaf of bread and devour it before a human can cross the kitchen. If there's anything more than a plastic bag left, that dog is slowing down.

TRAINING BELIEF

Faith is to believe what you do not see;
the reward of this faith is to see what you believe.

ST. AUGUSTINE

IT'S TRUE OF DOGS, TOO

The quickest way for a parent to get a child's
attention is to sit down and look comfortable.

LANE OLINGHOUSE

OBEDIENCE LESSON

True obedience is true freedom.

HENRY WARD BEECHER

TROPICAL VACATION?

In northern climates, on cold days, dogs love to
sleep near the radiator and heating vents.
Who knows if it's their version of a tropical
vacation, as they dream of running down a beach,
chasing a splendid bird.

DOGITUDE VERSUS CATTITUDE

If animals could speak, the dog would
be a blundering outspoken fellow; but the
cat would have the rare grace of never
saying a word too much.

MARK TWAIN

DOGGY DELIGHT

We may not successfully teach old dogs new tricks,
but they fit our lives as if they'd always been there.
They know our house rules and our personal quirks,
adore us, and ask only for a cozy bed, good food,
and a gentle pat. Who else delights in us for such
meager returns?

WHO'S IN CHARGE?

Then God said, "Let us make man in our image, in our likeness, and let them rule over the fish of the sea and the birds of the air, over the livestock, over all the earth, and over all the creatures that move along the ground."

GENESIS 1:26

THANKS, LORD!

Thank You, Lord, for giving me a dog who reminds me of the joy in life. When people depress me with bad news, my dog points out that there's still reason to remain cheerful: We still have each other and a good game of ball.

DEEP NEED

Dogs have a way of finding the people
who need them, filling an emptiness
we don't even know we have.

THOM JONES

APPRECIATION

It's nice to have a pet that offers unconditional love,
someone who doesn't talk back. I love cats, but cats
take you on their terms. My golden retriever could
have a broken leg, and his teeth could be falling out,
but if I walk in the door, he'll wag his tail until it hurts.

BOB VETERE

A LITTLE SMARTER

I used to look at [my dog] Smokey and think, "If you were a little smarter you could tell me what you were thinking," and he'd look at me like he was saying, "If you were a little smarter, I wouldn't have to."

FRED JUNGCLAUS

HUMAN/CANINE PSYCHOLOGY

Pet stores always put those low-slung bins where a dog can just reach into one and grab a bone or pig's ear. *How could I part him from it?* and, *It's already slobbered on*, the human thinks. The store owners have both human and hound psychology down pat!

SHARED LOVE

Whoever loveth me, loveth my hound.

THOMAS MORE

DOGGY TREAT

When a dog picks up a pig's ear, does he muse,
"If the ears are this good, I wonder what the rest of
this beast's like"?

DOG'S WALKING RULE

I'll walk where my own nature would be leading—
It vexes me to choose another guide.

EMILY BRONTË

INSIDE TRUTH

It's funny how dogs and cats know the insides of folks better than other folks do, isn't it?

ELEANOR H. PORTER

FOOD FOR WISDOM

Lord, before I had a dog, I never thought so much about what he should eat. Now I often think about his treats, scraps, and dog food. Help me feed my dog wisely and well—but not too much.

THE CURATE'S DOG

His long-tried friend, for they,
As well we knew, together had grown grey.
The Master died, his drooping servant's grief
Found at the Widow's feet some sad relief;
Yet still he lived in pining discontent,
Sadness which no indulgence could prevent.

WILLIAM WORDSWORTH

IMPERMANENCE

Frolic seems a puppy's permanent state, but too quickly dogs reach the sedateness of maturity and slowness of old age. Each time has its pleasures—for them and for us. We both must make the most of them.

COMING?

Dogs come when they're called. Cats take a message and get back to you.

MARY BLY

COST OF DOGS

Before you get a second dog, be sure you can afford vet and food bills and the time, during walks, for admiring people to stop and pet them both.

DOG-CARE COUNSEL

Put on then. . .compassionate hearts, kindness,
humility, meekness, and patience.

COLOSSIANS 3:12 ESV

CONVERSATION STARTER

To get dog lovers talking, ask them about their pups. In a moment they'll be smiling like proud parents, and you'll know every detail about both canines and humans.

SMELLING IS BELIEVING

For man, "seeing is believing." Well, for a dog,
smelling is believing. If she doesn't smell it,
she can't figure it out. It's not real to her. . . .
Dogs have the ability to sniff out smells that we
can't even pick up using sophisticated scientific
equipment.

CESAR MILLAN

END OF THE LEASH

Walk a dog who's in a hurry, and you'll wonder who's really at the *end* of the leash. After all, he's at one extremity, and you're at the other!

DOG-FOOD WARNING

Never eat more than you can lift.

MISS PIGGY

STEWARDSHIP

*Lord, You've given me this dog to care for. Help me
share the loving-kindness I've received from You.
Remind me, when I'm tired and cranky, that I'm
accountable to You for my care for him.*

PUPPY-FRUSTRATION HELP

Kindness is the ability to love someone more than
they deserve.

ANONYMOUS

ANIMAL WISDOM

Ask the beasts, and they will teach you;
and the birds of the air, and they will tell you. . .
that the hand of the LORD has done this,
in whose hand *is* the life of every living thing,
and the breath of all mankind?

JOB 12:7, 9–10 NKJV

YOUNG DOGS

Young dogs delight in constant motion and chewing, then a deep nap just about anywhere. Bowls full of food are gobbled down instantly and treats demanded constantly.

OLD DOGS

Old dogs delight in simple things: a soft bed,
a gentle hand on the head, and good food to eat
as slowly as possible. Add in a few special treats,
to be enjoyed at their leisure, and their day is made.

A DOG'S PERSPECTIVE

Eat a live toad the first thing in the morning and nothing worse will happen to you the rest of the day.

ANONYMOUS

CHILDHOOD FRIENDS

A deep love for dogs often comes out of our
childhood days. A youth shared with them gives
us an appreciation for dogs' listening ears and
faithful hearts. Secrets told to these companions
of our early days are never divulged.

SLEEP DENS

Wild dogs sleep in dens, and their domestic counterparts also favor a sheltered sleeping spot that feels like a den—hence the under-the-bed or under-the-table sleeping habits of many domestic dogs.

BEST BEHAVIOR

NOSE NEWS

A dog raises its nose to sniff the wind. Though we can't smell a thing, he breathes deeply, obviously delighting in information about the dog down the block, the local deli's specials, and the weather forecast. These scents are his newspaper and e-mail all in one.

THE WIND IN MY EARS

I can feel the wind go by when I run. It feels good.
It feels fast.

EVELYN ASHFORD

FINE DOGS

Any member introducing a dog into the
Society's premises shall be liable to a fine
of one pound. Any animal leading a blind
person shall be deemed to be a cat.

RULE 46, OXFORD UNION SOCIETY,
LONDON

JOY OF YOUTH

Joy will make a puppy of an old dog.

THORNTON W. BURGESS

BETTER BED

No matter how soft and expensive a bed you buy for the new puppy, your bed will always look better to her. If she shares your bedroom, just as you're drifting off to sleep, *tha-thump*, you'll hear her landing on your bed.

NECESSITY

Children and dogs are as necessary to the welfare of
the country as Wall Street and the railroads.

HARRY S. TRUMAN

THE BLIND HIGHLAND BOY

A dog too, had he; not for need,
But one to play with and to feed;
Which would have led him, if bereft
Of company or friends, and left
Without a better guide.

WILLIAM WORDSWORTH

GUARD TERRIER?

Punch loved everybody. . . . He was as cordial to a beggar as he would have been to a king; and if thieves had come to break through and steal, Punch. . .would have escorted them through the house, and shown them where the treasures were kept.

LAURENCE HUTTON

HUMILITY

I'm really getting a handle on this training thing, the new dog owner thinks. That's the moment when his dog decides to lie down in the middle of the road or bark outrageously at the terrier across the street. Every dog can instantaneously humble its human.

GOD'S SENSE OF HUMOR

The God who made giraffes, a baby's fingernails,
a puppy's tail, a crooknecked squash, the bobwhite's
call, and a young girl's giggle has a sense of humor.
Make no mistake about that.

CATHERINE MARSHALL

PRAYER CORRAL

Let God's Word and God's love
be the herd dogs chasing your
thoughts into the prayer corral.

CHUCK MILLER

DOGGY DELIGHT

Four feet straight up in the air, back in the lush green grass, a wiggle or two of delight. What more can a dog ask of life—unless it's to have her human on the other end of the leash?

DOG TALK

Dogs do speak, but only to those who know how to listen.

ORHAN PAMUK

REMINDER

Some of us look admiringly at long-haired dogs but
know we're unlikely to spend hours grooming them.
Yet twice a year our own short-haired dogs remind
us that they, too, are long on fur as they shed
enough of it to cover a couple of canines.

SPECIES DIFFERENCES

Confront a child, a puppy, and a kitten with a
sudden danger; the child will turn instinctively
for assistance, the puppy will grovel in abject
submission, the kitten will brace its tiny
body for a frantic resistance.

SAKI

FRIENDLY ADVICE

Harry S. Truman, who is reported to have said, "If you want a friend in Washington, get a dog," briefly owned a cocker spaniel named Feller, given to him as a Christmas gift. Instead of keeping his Washington friend, he gave him away to his doctor.

DACHSIE DEFINITION

Dachshund: A half-a-dog high and a dog-and-a-half long.

HENRY LOUIS MENCKEN

THE COST

We dog lovers may go walking in the rain because the dog enjoys it or stay awake all night with an ill dog. In response, our dogs warm us in snowy weather and cuddle us nightlong when insomnia strikes. For both of us, it's a relationship that's not without cost.

CANINE FRIENDSHIP ATTITUDE

Strangers are just friends waiting to happen.

ANONYMOUS

A DOG'S MONIKER

Naming a dog is an awesome thing. You must be able to shout the moniker with ease and without embarrassment. It must suit your dog throughout his years. Best choice? Wait a few days and let the dog tell you his name.

Really, he will.

WALKLESS

If it wasn't for dogs, some people would never go for a walk.

ANONYMOUS

CLEANING DAY

What is better for clearing off a crowded table than the long tail of a tall dog or for keeping socks and shoes put away than a teething puppy?

NEXT-DOOR DOG CHALLENGE

The entire law is summed
up in a single command:
"Love your neighbor as yourself."

GALATIANS 5:14

UNCRITICAL AFFECTION

We long for an affection altogether ignorant of our faults. Heaven has accorded this to us in the uncritical canine attachment.

GEORGE ELIOT

UGLY-DOG TRUTH

Sometimes the heart sees what is invisible to the eye.

H. JACKSON BROWN JR.

FAITHFUL FRIEND

Greyfriars Bobby, a Skye terrier, accompanied his policeman owner daily on his rounds in Edinburgh. Following the death of his master, Bobby habitually lay on John Gray's grave for fourteen years. He was fed by the people of the town and licensed by the city's Lord Provost.

I BARK

A dog's bark is as much a signature as its scent.
Every bark is a full, clear statement of existence—
"I bark, therefore I am." It is unrestrained,
unedited, and unabashed.

JOHN O'HURLEY

FUR COUNT

Lord, thank You for the deep dog–human bond. May people who have lost their beloved companions be comforted by Your deep love and know that not one bit of fur was uncounted by You.

ALMOST HUMAN

We treat our dogs as if they were "almost human": that is why they really become "almost human" in the end.

C. S. LEWIS

NAMING DAY

Now the LORD God had formed out of the ground
all the beasts of the field and all the birds of the air.
He brought them to the man to see what he would
name them; and whatever the man called each living
creature, that was its name.

GENESIS 2:19

WHY BOTHER?

You may have a dog that won't sit up,
roll over or even cook breakfast,
not because she's too stupid to learn how
but because she's too smart to bother.

RICK HOROWITZ

PUPPY PARENTING ADVICE

Puppy parenting is not about buying the best of everything. It is about providing the best care and giving lots of love.

JAN GREYE AND GAIL SMITH WITH BEVERLY BEYETTE

DOG'S WISH

I want to walk through life instead of being dragged through it.

ALANIS MORISSETTE

HOME ALONE

Don't you wonder just what your dogs do when
they're home alone? Do they sleep on the forbidden
couch, chew on a toy, or climb onto the table? Or
maybe they curl up in their own beds or in the
hallway and dream of your return.

COMMANDMENT TO DOGS

People are unreasonable, illogical,
and self-centered. Love them anyway.

ANONYMOUS

BLESSED MEMORIES

After we lose a dog to death, God leaves us with a lifetime of memories: bright, active, sunlit days and dull, rainy ones with hound and human warming by the fire. We never forget that canine who shared our lives; we can always feel blessed by the gift of time we shared.

DOG PSYCHOLOGY

A vigorous five-mile walk will do more good for an unhappy, but otherwise healthy adult than all the medicine and psychology in the world.

PAUL DUDLEY WHITE

DOG-BOWL EXPERTISE

Mix two types of food into a dog's bowl, and she can always nose out the less-favored type with deadly accuracy. Not only does she have an amazing nose that can identify each bit, but with just a tongue and nose, she separates them exactly.

BEST FOOD?

I don't eat anything that a dog won't eat.
Like sushi. Ever see a dog eat sushi?
He just sniffs it and says, "I don't think so."
And this is an animal that licks between
its legs and sniffs fire hydrants.

BILLIAM CORONEL

FRIENDSHIP

Though my dog is my best friend, Lord, may he never be my only friend. Help me to build relationships with other dog lovers, in the dog park, on walks, and by sharing the joys of having a dog with others.

BLESSING FOR A RESCUED DOG

Always remember to forget the
things that made you sad.
But never forget to remember
the things that made you glad.
Always remember to forget the
friends that proved untrue.
But never forget to remember
those who have stuck by you.

IRISH BLESSING

SNOW DOG

What is more amusing than a dog's frenetic romp in the snow? It's as if God made the weather just for her, and she has to get the most out of it.

WORKING-DOG'S BELIEF

Action may not always bring happiness. . .
but there is no happiness without action.

BENJAMIN DISRAELI

GOOD BREEDER

Need to find a good dog breeder? Look for one who asks many questions and has a contract stating that the dog must be returned to the breeder if it needs to be re-homed.

CUTE PUPS

There are all sorts of cute puppy dogs, but it doesn't stop people from going out and buying Dobermans.

ANGUS YOUNG

DISOBEDIENCE

When our dogs don't obey, God's given us a life-size picture of our relationship with Him. Through man's best friend, we see the generous care He pours out on us, just because He loves us.

SCENT CHALLENGED

They haven't got no noses,
The fallen sons of Eve;
Even the smell of roses
Is not what they supposes;
But more than mind discloses
And more than men believe.

G. K. CHESTERTON

PUPPY WARNING

Look at that cute mutt puppy's paws before you take him home. Large paws mean a large dog in the making. Don't be fooled by the fact that he fits so well in your arms today—tomorrow he may stand as high as your dining-room table.

WISELY MADE

How many are your works, O LORD! In wisdom you made them all; the earth is full of your creatures.

PSALM 104:24

FENCING

Fences are great for keeping dogs in a yard, but only if the humans remember to close the gate!

MRS. DINGLEY'S DOG'S TAG

Pray steal me not, I'm Mrs. Dingley's,
Whose heart in this
four-footed thing lies.

JONATHAN SWIFT

TO MY SENIOR FOSTER

Thank you for curling up on my chair,
  trusting me though others failed you so.
From now on, you will never lack a friend
  and will always have a place to go.

A DOG'S APOLOGIES

Master, this is Thy Servant.
He is rising eight weeks old.
He is mainly Head and Tummy.
His legs are uncontrolled.
But Thou hast forgiven his ugliness,
And settled him on Thy knee. . .
Art Thou content with Thy Servant?
He is very comfy with Thee.

RUDYARD KIPLING

PACK MENTALITY

Though we don't look at all like them, dogs accept us as part of their pack. Our weaknesses—small, feeble ears and noses, two legs, and a distinct lack of fur—don't keep them from loving us.

DOG'S TRAVEL ADVICE

Stop worrying about the potholes
in the road and celebrate the journey!

BARBARA HOFFMAN

FORGIVENESS

Lord, my dog may not be perfect, but I still love her. Help me to encourage her and focus on the things she does right. Remind me, as anger threatens, that when I fail, You still love me.

DOG AND BOY

A little Dog that wags his tail
And knows no other joy
Of such a little Dog am I
Reminded by a Boy

Who gambols all the living Day
Without an earthly cause
Because he is a little Boy
I honestly suppose.

EMILY DICKINSON

LAPDOG QUESTION

Why is it that people who give up on training a large dog and send him to a shelter usually manage to teach him to be a lapdog before they let him go?

HOMECOMING

'Tis sweet to hear the watch dog's honest bark
Bay deep-mouthed welcome
as we draw near home;
'Tis sweet to know there is an eye will mark
Our coming and look brighter when we come.

LORD BYRON

APPRECIATION

Lord, I give my dog a simple dog treat, and he acts as if he's received a five-course dinner. May I be that appreciative of the ordinary, good things You give me.

CANINE NAPPING THEORY

No day is so bad it can't be fixed with a nap.

CARRIE SNOW

DON'T LAUGH!

Do not laugh at a large, burly man's tenderness for a small dog. Love for those who are weaker is a sign of true strength.

SMART DOG

There is only one smartest dog in the world,
and every boy has it.

ANONYMOUS

WALK IN THE PARK

It may not be a walk in the park to regularly exercise a dog, but a well-walked dog is less likely to cause trouble. A healthy dog gets enough exercise to make him happily tired.

DOG WASH

Anybody who doesn't know what soap tastes like
never washed a dog.

FRANKLIN P. JONES

OPTIMISM

Humans seem to believe a dog can be house-trained in two days. Dogs hope the humans will have patience for as long as it takes.

HOMEBODY HOUND

What is more agreeable than one's home?

MARCUS TULLIUS CICERO

RESCUE QUESTIONS

Why would anyone give up this wonderful dog? rescuers often wonder. Just because a dog has lost its home doesn't mean there's something wrong with it. Often there was a problem in the humans' lives.

ENTERING THE ARK

Pairs of all creatures that have the breath of life
in them came to Noah and entered the ark.
The animals going in were male and female of
every living thing, as God had commanded Noah.
Then the LORD shut him in.

GENESIS 7:15–16

COMMON SENSE

A human can spend years trying to train a dog not to chew on shoes and the TV remote, or can simply put them out of his reach. After all, which of the two is supposed to have common sense?

THE CANINE GOURMAND

There is no sincerer love than the love of food.

George Bernard Shaw

LONG-EARED ALERT

How can ears flopped over toward the ground so swiftly hear the voice of a loved one half a block away? Shouldn't alert ears, pointed toward the sun, hear more than those that need to lift aside to hear the same sound?

A LONELY DOG'S LAMENT

When you depart from me sorrow abides,
and happiness takes his leave.

William Shakespeare

PLEASE!

Every dog knows how to make the most of its soulful look. Large, round eyes stare into the human's face with a begging expression. Only a powerful person can deny this pitiful view of the dog's innermost being.

ON MILLIE'S AMAZING PUBLISHING SUCCESS

Study hard, and you might grow up to be president. But let's face it: Even then, you'll never make as much money as your dog.

GEORGE H. W. BUSH

INSTANTANEOUS BED

Drop a towel, quilt, pillows, or bedsheets on the floor, and a dog will easily decide it's a wonderful, soft bed that has the additional quality of smelling just like her favorite human.

WATCHDOG WARNING

It's a poor watchdog who sleeps with both eyes closed.

THORNTON W. BURGESS

THE DOG PARTY

Leaping, loping, four abreast, they came plunging like so many North Winds to their party! Streak of Snow—Glow of Fire—Frozen Mud—Sun-Spot!—Yelping-mouthed—slapping-tailed! Backs bristling! Legs stiffening! Wolf Hound, Setter, Bull Dog, Dalmatian—each according to his kind, hurtling, crowding!

ELEANOR HALLOWELL ABBOTT

WHERE TO STOP?

Why own a dog? There's a danger you know,
You can't own just one, for the craving will grow.
There's no doubt they're addictive,
wherein lies the danger.
While living with lots, you'll grow
poorer and stranger.

ANONYMOUS

SMILE!

Do dogs smile? Maybe, maybe not. But no matter what its mouth looks like, every dog can bring a smile to a human face.

A WORKING-DOG'S THOUGHT

Everyone enjoys doing the kind of work for which he is best suited.

NAPOLEON HILL

WET DOG

Why does a wet dog immediately head for the humans' bed or couch? Do dogs see them as some species of huge, thick towels?

HEART AIM

A dog has one aim in life. . .to bestow his heart.

J. R. ACKERLEY

SKIN DEEP

Dogs with spotted coats also have spotted skin; their coat pattern is repeated at skin level. But dogs can also change color as they age—that black spot on a tricolor puppy may turn brown when he's an adult.

BACK-DOOR POOCH HOPE

Ask, and it will be given to you; seek, and you
will find; knock, and it will be opened to you.
For everyone who asks receives, and he who seeks
finds, and to him who knocks it will be opened.

MATTHEW 7:7–8 NKJV

BELLY RUBS

The delight of a good belly rub can hardly be overestimated for either the human or the dog. For the dog, it's pure physical joy. To a human, it's a sign of the dog's deep trust and affection.

SQUISHED-IN FACES

Bulldogs are adorable, with faces
like toads that have been sat on.

COLETTE

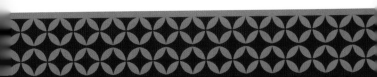

TABLE MANNERS

When cats jump on tables at mealtime, it's a real irritant. But when dogs do it, dinner is history—it's immediately inside a wet, possibly slobbery mouth, and no one except the dog wants it anymore.

CAR RIDE

Dogs feel very strongly that they should always go with you in the car, in case the need should arise for them to bark violently at nothing right in your ear.

DAVE BARRY

ONE-DOG NIGHT

On a somewhat cold night, there is nothing as cozy as a large dog lying at your feet—preferably under the covers. By morning, however, you'll often have thrown every cover off the bed, because you're both so warm.

COMMON GROUND

How very unlike are poodles and greyhounds!
Yet they are of one species.

ADAM SEDGWICK

"HOME" OR "HOMEOWNER"?

"Home is where the heart is" until the humans walk out the door. That's when the dog begins to realize that part of the pack is gone. The howling that results may be terrible to hear!

MEETING SIEGFRIED'S DOGS

The upper half of the door was of glass and, as I peered through, a river of dogs poured round the corner of a long passage and dashed itself with frenzied yells against the door. If I hadn't been used to animals I would have turned and run for my life.

JAMES HERRIOT

TRUE TO LIFE

Dodie Smith, author of the book that formed the basis for the Disney movie *101 Dalmatians*, named the canine hero after her first Dalmatian, Pongo. The scene where a puppy was revived shortly after birth came from an experience with a litter born to two of her Dalmatians.

TED

I have a little brindle dog,
Seal-brown from tail to head.
His name I guess is Theodore,
But I just call him Ted. . . .

He plays around about the house,
As good as he can be,
He don't seem like a little dog,
He's just like folks to me.

MAXINE ANNA BUCK

CONFUSING SIGNS?

Accessible TV remotes seem to be a sign, to the dog, that their humans love them. The two-leggers leave this tempting object that smells just like them within reach of canine jaws.

PUPPY'S FRIENDSHIP KEY

The only way to have a friend is to be one.

RALPH WALDO EMERSON

BULLDOGS ALL

Thirty-nine universities have bulldogs as their mascot. Among them are Uga, of the University of Georgia; Bully, at Mississippi State; Handsome Dan the XVII, of Yale; and Jack at Georgetown.

MY DOG

If dogs were fashioned out of men
What breed of dog would I have been?
And would I e'er deserve caress,
Or be extolled for faithfulness
Like my dog here?

JOSEPH M. ANDERSON

WHADDAYACALLIT?

Having a hard time naming your new pup?
Go online and you'll find plenty of Web sites that
will help you out. You can choose a name for your
dog from any number of languages, including Latin.

MY DOGGIE

My doggie is unquestionably the most charming, and. . .delightful doggie that ever was born. . .my doggie is unique, a perfectly beautiful and singular specimen of—of well, I won't say what, because my friends usually laugh at me when I say it.

R. M. BALLANTYNE

GO WITH THE FLOW

*Lord, I know my dog was bred for a certain purpose,
and I can't change those inbred traits, no matter how
hard I try. Help me to accept those things I can't change,
develop his good points, and love him no matter what.*

INCREDIBLE DOG

When you think about it, dogs are incredible
creatures. In a short time, they can learn an
amazing amount of our human language. . .
they have the capacity to intuit our moods,
read our facial expressions, and find
meaning in our body language.

BASH DIBRA

TREATS

Clearly, dogs believe every day should include at least one treat, whether it's a long walk in the park or a tasty bone. They know how to appreciate the simple but good things in life.

GREETINGS

Labradors are lousy watchdogs. They usually
bark when there is a stranger about, but it is
an expression of unmitigated joy at the
chance to meet somebody new, not a warning.

NORMAN STRUNG

LEARNING EXPERIENCE

Patience: That quality of long-suffering a human may not have when he gets a stubborn dog, but that surely will develop over time as the dog completes its people-training program.

DIVERSION

Cat's Motto: No matter what you've done wrong,
always try to make it look like the dog did it.

ANONYMOUS

VIDEO STARS

For Christmas 2005, the White House produced the
video "A Very Beazley Christmas." Miss Beazley,
the Scottish terrier President George W. Bush had
bought for his wife that year, received so much
attention and praise that their first Scottie, Barney,
jealously began hiding Beazley's Christmas presents.

SAD LAD

Lad did not belong to the howling type. When he was unhappy, he waxed silent. And his sorrowful eyes took on a deeper woe. By the way, if there is anything more sorrowful than the eyes of a collie pup that has never known sorrow, I have yet to see it.

Albert Payson Terhune

I CAN'T EAR YOU!

According to the *Guinness Book of World Records*, an American bloodhound named Tigger has the longest dog ears on record. Each of these amazing appendages is well over thirteen inches in length.

LEADING CANINE

Some of my best leading men
have been dogs and horses.

ELIZABETH TAYLOR

LOW DOWN

From the lowly perspective of a dog's eyes,
everyone looks short.

Proverb

GREATEST TREASURES

A puppy has an unerring ability to identify your greatest treasures. That's how she knows to chew on your favorite pair of shoes, the table a family member made for you, and the cookbook with the best recipes, or the mystery with the best plot.

SOURCE OF SPARKY'S JOY?

Those who bring sunshine into the lives of others cannot keep it from themselves.

JAMES M. BARRIE

THE PERFECT DACHSHUND

My name is Stumps, and my mistress is rather
a nice little girl; but she has her faults,
like most people. I myself, as it happens,
am wonderfully free from faults.

EDITH NESBIT

EVERYDAY MONGREL

I like a bit of a mongrel myself, whether it's a man or a dog. They're the best for everyday.

George Bernard Shaw

TRAINING MOMENT

A well-trained dog is a lifelong pleasure. Thank You, Lord, for keeping me patient in teaching my dog how we can share a safe, happy, and loving life. May I always faithfully show my dog the best way to live.

LEARNING POINT

Whether the Creator planned it so, or environment
and human companionship have made it so,
men may learn richly through the love and fidelity
of a brave and devoted dog.

WARREN G. HARDING

ONE OF A KIND

Like humans, each dog is distinctive.
One hates walking in the rain, while another
can't wait to jump in the pool. It's often just
the way of this world that the owner with
the pool gets the dog who hates being wet.

TOO HUMAN?

It was the Great Creator himself who made dogs too human—so human that sometimes they put humanity to shame.

LAURENCE HUTTON

OUR FRIEND THE DOG

He loves us not only in his consciousness and
his intelligence: the very instinct of his race, the
entire unconsciousness of his species, it appears,
think only of us, dream only of being useful to us.

MAURICE MAETERLINCK

A DOG'S TAIL

The motion of [a dog's tail] is full of meaning.
There is the slow wag of anger; the gentle wag of
contentment; the brisker wag of joy: and what can
be more mutely expressive than the limp states of
sorrow, humility, and fear?

ALFRED ELWES

WARNING SIGNAL

"Beware, beware" warns the barking dog, alerting his humans to the dire threats of a squirrel in the yard or a passing pedestrian. Who else would care for such small "enemies" in our lives? If only he could also alert mankind to the enemies of pride, hatred, and wickedness.

WARNING SIGNAL

Beware of the man who does not talk, and the dog that does not bark.

CHEYENNE PROVERB

MULTIPLE-DOG DILEMMA

Can two walk together, except they be agreed?

AMOS 3:3 KJV

CANINE NAPPING PHILOSOPHY

Seek home for rest, for home is best.

THOMAS TUSSER

GENTLEMAN DOG

To call him a dog hardly seems to do him justice,
though inasmuch as he had four legs, a tail,
and barked, I admit he was, to all outward
appearances. But to those of us who knew
him well, he was a perfect gentleman.

HERMIONE GINGOLD

SHARING

Muddy-pawed dogs always seem to walk on the lightest-colored carpeting or furniture the humans have in the house. To a canine, it makes perfect sense: Shouldn't the humans get to share this wonderful weather?

CANINE PHILOSOPHY

No philosophers so thoroughly comprehend us as dogs and horses.

HERMAN MELVILLE

A MUTT'S QUALITIES

As terrier he would dig furiously by the hour after a field mouse; as spaniel he would "read" the breeze with the best nose among the dog folk of our neighborhood, or follow a trail quite well.

HARRY ESTY DOUNCE

CAREER OPTION

I sometimes think I'd rather be a dog
and bay at the moon than stay in the
Senate another six years and listen to it.

SENATOR JOHN SHARP WILLIAMS

CHARMING COMMAND?

"Stay" is a charming word in a friend's vocabulary.

LOUISA MAY ALCOTT

HOME AND LOVE

Lord, I often hear about dogs who don't have homes.
Help me do my part to help those homeless companions
find the people who will love them.

DOGS WILL BARK

Dogs do always bark at those they know not,
and. . .it is their nature to accompany one
another in those clamors.

SIR WALTER RALEIGH

RESCUE'S SECURITY

I'll be good, really! pleaded the rescue dog's eyes. You take him home, shower him with affection, train him in your ways. In time, he finally feels loved. One day he empties the trash can on your floor, breaks into the dog treats, and chews six rolls of toilet paper. Congratulations, you've bonded!

SOFT SPOT FOR SPOT

To my way of thinking there's something wrong, or missing, with any person who hasn't got a soft spot in their heart for an animal of some kind.

WILL JAMES

DOGS AS CHILDREN

What dogs? These are my children, little people
with fur who make my heart open a little wider.

OPRAH WINFREY

A NEW PUPPY

Archie's seven-week-old St. Bernard puppy has come and it is the dearest puppy imaginable; a huge, soft thing, which Archie carries around in his arms and which the whole family loves.

THEODORE ROOSEVELT

DAYTIME WALKIES?

Walk while you have the light, lest darkness
overtake you; he who walks in darkness
does not know where he is going.

JOHN 12:35 NKJV

HOLD MY HAND

Lord, be with us as we go to the vet today. I'm thankful for my dog's good health and concerned for her well-being. Hold my hand, even as I hold her leash.

EARTHLY BEAUTY

Ask of the beasts and they will teach you the beauty of this earth.

FRANCIS OF ASSISI

PUPPY LOVE

[Being a parent] is tough. If you just want a
wonderful little creature to love, you can get a puppy.

BARBARA WALTERS

CHOW HOUND

Though your dog may chow down on anything set before him, try to feed him the best food you can reasonably afford. You'll spend less in vet bills, and your dog is likely to live longer if he eats well.

FRACTIOUS DOG'S OUTLOOK

One of the advantages of being disorderly is that
one is constantly making exciting discoveries.

A. A. MILNE

LOVE YOUR DOG

A righteous man has regard for the life of his animal.

PROVERBS 12:10 NASB

PUG'S NAP

Before her home, in her accustom'd seat,
The tidy Grandam spins beneath the shade
Of the old honeysuckle, at her feet
The dreaming pug, and purring tabby laid.

FREDERICK TENNYSON

GOD'S GIFT

Puppies are lively gifts from God. After they've been reprimanded for chewing the doorjamb, forgetting their training, and awakening us early in the morning, let's remember that they'll turn around, ready for a delightful rough-and-tumble session of play—and we may be their favorite play companions.

LITERARY ANIMAL

It is true that animals play an important role in prose fiction, more important than is often realized, for a book without animals is seldom a living book.

CARL VAN VECHTEN

HUMAN–DOG
COMMON GROUND

Food is our common ground, a universal experience.

JAMES BEARD

OBEDIENCE TRAINING

It is verily a great thing to live in obedience, to be under authority, and not to be at our own disposal. Far safer is it to live in subjection than in a place of authority.

THOMAS À KEMPIS

HUMAN-DOG LOVE

The heart that has truly loved never forgets,
but as truly loves on to the close.

Thomas More

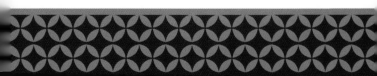

GAINING OBEDIENCE

Trying to force a dog to obey commands is an exercise in futility, but a few special treats and a simple word of instruction can do the job in short order.

GOD'S FOOD PROMISE

He giveth to the beast his food, and to the young ravens which cry.

PSALM 147:9 KJV

A SUMMER WALK

In summer, when the days were long,
We walk'd, two friends, in field and wood;
Our heart was light, our step was strong,
And life lay round us, fair as good,
In summer, when the days were long.

WATHEN MARKS WILKS CALL

HOUND OF THE BASKERVILLES

A hound it was, an enormous
coal-black hound, but not such a
hound as mortal eyes have ever seen.
Fire burst from its open mouth,
its eyes glowed with a smouldering glare,
its muzzle and hackles and dewlap
were outlined in flickering flame.

SIR ARTHUR CONAN DOYLE

CANINE COMFORT

Nothing comforts a hurting human heart like a slurpy dog kiss and a long, furry, canine cuddle. And what human shares our list of troubles without complaint, even when we've repeated it for the thousandth time?

LION DOG

A Pekingese is not a pet dog; he is an undersized lion.

A. A. MILNE

LADY TRAMP

The dog who served as a model for Walt Disney's Tramp in *Lady and the Tramp*, was actually a lady. Disney bailed this female stray out of the city pound after she was spotted at the studio, then disappeared. She lived out her days at Disneyland.

MEETING MUNGO

[Mungo] was a medium-sized dog, nothing special, a hound of some sort, the kind you'd pick out at the shelter to adopt, flop-eared, tan and white coat, immediately likeable, the kind of dog you itched to scratch between the ears.

MARTHA GRIMES

LOST DOG

A man running for office puts me in mind of a dog that's lost—he smells everybody he meets, and wags himself all over.

JOSH BILLINGS

WEIGHT PROBLEM

If your dog is fat, you're not getting enough exercise.

ANONYMOUS

PUPPY LOVE?

Craving a puppy? Think twice. Older dogs often come house-trained and are more likely to do well when left alone for hours. Many will also do better with young children. A somewhat older dog who needs a home will also never forget what you've done for him.

DOGGY PLAY CONCEPT

Never put off till tomorrow
the fun you can have today.

Aldous Huxley

HOW THE DOG GOT LOST

If you don't know where you are going, any road will get you there.

LEWIS CARROLL

ENJOY LIFE!

All of the animals except man know that the
principal business of life is to enjoy it.

Samuel Butler

PACK BELIEF

He who barks last, barks best.

DOG'S NAP

Oh sleep
It is a gentle thing,
Beloved from pole to pole.

SAMUEL TAYLOR COLERIDGE

REALIZATION

Old age means realizing you will never own all the dogs you wanted to.

JOE GORES

HOMELESS PUPS

When I see an ad showing a hurting pup, my heart reaches out, Lord. I understand why some people end up taking in more animals than they can care for. But help me to be wise in caring, however many dogs I own.

VISUAL POWER

An animal's eyes have the power to speak a great language.

MARTIN BUBER

MORNING EXERCISE

An early-morning walk is a
blessing for the whole day.

HENRY DAVID THOREAU

SHARED AFFECTION

I've caught more ills from people sneezing over me and giving me virus infections than from kissing dogs.

BARBARA WOODHOUSE

SLEEPY-DOG ATTITUDE

Laziness is nothing more than the habit of resting before you get tired.

JULES RENARD

WALK TIME

No squirrel went abroad;
A dog's belated feet
Like intermittent plush were heard
Adown the empty street.

EMILY DICKINSON

LOST DOG

Prevention is the best way to keep a dog safe.
But anyone who loses a dog should initially focus
the search on a mile-wide radius about the place it
was lost. Most dogs are found within that area.

DOG'S FAVORITE SPOT

I love it, I love it, and who shall dare
To chide me for loving that old arm-chair?

ELIZA COOK

ELECTION REQUIREMENT?

Any man who does not like dogs and want them
about does not deserve to be in the White House.

CALVIN COOLIDGE

SPEAK!

A dog can learn up to about one hundred sixty-five words. Some are bound to be the ones you'd rather not have him understand! If a dog gets overly excited at a word that indicates an upcoming pleasure, change, spell, or abbreviate it.

MORE FAITHFUL?

There is no one in all the Great World
more faithful than a faithful dog.

THORNTON W. BURGESS

TAKE A WALK

Golf seems to be an arduous way to go for a walk.
I prefer to take the dogs out.

PRINCESS ANNE

RESCUE ME!

Rescue a tail-wagger from a terrible situation, and she's likely to adore you lifelong. If it's a family rescue, she's most likely to connect most strongly with the first person who shows her affection.

A DOG'S SPRINGTIME JOY

In the spring, at the end of the day, you should smell like dirt.

MARGARET ATWOOD

A PUPPY'S DEFINITION

Leash: A long, weblike device that allows a dog to control his human and pull her in the opposite direction of where she would otherwise go.

FAITHFUL FRIEND

Old dog Tray's ever faithful;
Grief can not drive him away;
He is gentle, he is kind—
shall never, never find
A better friend than old dog Tray!

STEPHEN COLLINS FOSTER

HOW TO LOVE A DOG

Have a heart that never hardens, and a temper that never tires, and a touch that never hurts.

CHARLES DICKENS

GENETIC PREDISPOSITION

Herding breeds often don't care what they round up, as long as they get to practice the job they were bred for. That may even mean herding the human children in their pack.

REMEMBERING GEIST

We stroke thy broad brown paws again,
We bid thee to thy vacant chair,
We greet thee by the window-pane,
We hear thy scuffle on the stair.

MATTHEW ARNOLD

NICKNAMES

Most dog people end up giving their animals
multiple nicknames. These may include an
abbreviation of the dog's name, a description of a
quirk, and at least one silly name (maybe that's why
they call them "pet names").

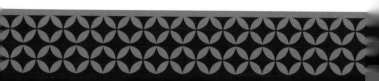

SLEEPING DOG

"Let a sleeping dog lie." It is a poor old maxim, and nothing in it: anybody can do it, you don't have to employ a dog.

MARK TWAIN

HUMAN'S BLISS

What bliss it is to rub the soft fur atop the ear of a long-eared hound or gently touch the tender fur of a puppy.

ONE-PERSON DOG

Dogs will be fairly indifferent to most
people and pick one, and say,
"That's the person I'll work for."

NINA BONDARENKO

LASKA'S MASTER'S RETURN

Laska kept poking her head under his hand.
He stroked her, and she promptly curled up at his
feet, laying her head on a hind-paw. And in token
of all now being well and satisfactory, she opened
her mouth a little, smacked her lips, and. . .sank into
blissful repose.

LEO TOLSTOY

DOG TOYS

There are two kinds of dog toys: the one that lasts for years because your dog loves it so much she treats it gently, and the one that is so vigorously chewed, it only lasts an hour. Who's to say which gives more enjoyment?

FLEA SEASON

In flea time it seemed hardly possible that a dog
of his size could sustain his population. . . . [Fleas]
don't relish every human; me they did; I used to
storm at him for it, and he used, between spasms of
scratching, to listen admiringly and wag.

HARRY ESTY DOUNCE

SMART DOG

Why, that dog is practically a Phi Beta Kappa.
She can sit up and beg, and she can give her paw.
I don't say she will but she can.

DOROTHY PARKER

SCENTS OF SMELL

"Smelling isn't everything," said the Elephant.

"Why," said the Bulldog, "if a fellow can't trust his nose, what is he to trust?"

"Well, his brains perhaps," she replied mildly.

C. S. Lewis

BEST BARK

A good Hound never barks on a cold trail.

THORNTON W. BURGESS

WIDE RANGE

No matter how big the dog bowl is, a long-eared,
deep-flewed dog never keeps water inside the bowl.
Instead, he shares it with the floors and walls.
If he shakes his head, his humans may even find
themselves cleaning the ceiling.

BARKING-DOG RELIEF

Whenever I hear a dog continually barking,
my reaction is one of relief—that it's not my dog
making all that racket and inciting the
neighbors to call the police.

John McCarthy

A RESCUER'S PRAYER

Lord, I wish I could wrap my arms around every dog that needs a home. Help me rescue every dog I can and to remember that You hold them all fast, because they all come from Your arms.

PUPPY RULE

Puppies need toys as much as kids do, and they
should learn that it's good to pick up and play—
as roughly as they want—with these toys and not
with hands. Hands are for stroking, petting,
and for making your dog feel good, not for chewing.

JOHN C. WRIGHT WITH JUDI WRIGHT LASHNITS

CANINE EMOTIONS

As much as any animal on earth, dogs express emotions as purely and clearly as a five-year-old child, and surely that's part of why we love them so much.

PATRICIA B. MCCONNELL

RELATIONAL TRUTH

The relationships between man and dog can often be as complex as that between man and woman. We have, own, or are owned by dogs for a great variety of reasons, not all of them exactly to our credit. We all want to be loved.

IAN NIALL

TIED UP?

Constantly chain a dog to a tree, and he'll become vicious. Loosely knot him to a heart, and faithful love will earn his adoration.

PUPPY LOVE

The best and most beautiful things in the world cannot be seen or even touched—they must be felt with the heart.

HELEN KELLER

MEMORY-LANE TEST

Doubt that a dog has a long memory? Take one back to a vet's office where he's experienced pain and try to get him in the door and settled, or take him to a dog park where he's had lots of fun and drag him home too soon.

PUPPY-PROOFING A HOUSE

Although you may feel a little silly, it's well
worth going round every room in the house
on all fours, to see exactly what is within
reach of an inquisitive, playful puppy!

DAVID TAYLOR

HOW'S TRICKS?

Dogs need to do something. They want to feel useful. They love to work for praise and to feel accomplished. Sitting around and decorating the hearth isn't quite enough. Tricks can be a useful and entertaining addition to your dog's education.

CAPTAIN ARTHUR J. HAGGERTY AND
CAROL LEA BENJAMIN

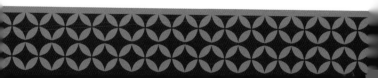

DOG SENSES

Dogs don't see much color, but let an object move, and they may be after it with incredible accuracy. And while dinner's cooking on the stove, if they could speak, dogs could accurately identify every ingredient the human put in the pot.

DIGGING IT

Most puppies, at one time or another, will have a go at landscape gardening. Leave your puppy outside on his own for long periods and he will get into mischief, just as a toddler would.

TERRY RYAN AND THERESA SHIPP

TRAINING ADVICE

Be prepared in season and out of season;
correct, rebuke and encourage—
with great patience and careful instruction.

2 TIMOTHY 4:2

COLLIE GIFTS

His mistress once praised him for bringing home
a pretty lace handkerchief he had found on
the highway. Until I forbade any further gifts,
[Sunnybank Robert] bore to her every roadside
offering he could find: a car crank, an umbrella
with a Chinese sword handle, a devastatingly dead
chicken, and an equally flattened skunk.

ALBERT PAYSON TERHUNE

A DOG'S LEARNING CURVE

It was necessary. . .to convince yourself that it is vain to pursue birds who fly away and that you are unable to clamber up trees after the cats who defy you there; to distinguish between the sunny spots where it is delicious to sleep and the patches of shade in which you shiver.

MAURICE MAETERLINCK

DESIGNER GENES

There are AKC-recognized breeds, designer dogs, and pure mutts. But all trace their lineage back to the first canines. The genetics of the multitude of breeds we have today lay in two sets of complex genes. What an amazing God He is who designed all that in a pair of animals.

THE IRISH WOLFHOUND

As fly the shadows o'er the grass,
He flies with step as light and sure,
He hunts the wolf through Tostan pass,
And starts the deer by Lisanoure.
The music of the Sabbath bells,
O Con! has not a sweeter sound
Than when along the valley swells
The cry of John MacDonnell's hound.

DENIS FLORENCE MACCARTHY

MORE VALUABLE DOGS

But now they that are younger than I have me in derision, whose fathers I would have disdained to have set with the dogs of my flock.

Job 30:1 kjv

EDUCATED CANINE?

For though he had very little Latin beyond "Cave canem [beware of the dog]," he had, as a young dog, devoured Shakespeare (in a tasty leather binding).

DODIE SMITH

THE BEST WE CAN BE

Dogs make us believe we can actually be as they see us.

THE MONKS OF NEW SKETE

DOG ALARM CLOCK

Once your new dog gets used to your schedule, don't be surprised if he wakes you in the morning. Canines don't need a clock to know what hour it is.

LARGE SOUL

Folk will know how large your soul is, by the way you treat a dog.

CHARLES F. DORAN

DO DOGS LOVE US?

Love is like the wind, you can't see it but you can feel it.

NICHOLAS SPARKS

FIRST CANINE CELEBRITY

Warren G. Harding's Airedale terrier, Laddie Boy, became a news celebrity and an integral part of the White House scene. He came to his new home the day after his master's inauguration and lived in the White House living quarters, not the kennels.

MOST FAITHFUL

Of the animals who live with us, many are
worthy of recognition, and more than all the
others and most faithful to man is the dog.

PLINY THE ELDER

TOWN MUTT

Ellie. . .a shaggy brown Disney-cute mutt, was the West Hebron town dog. She wandered from one house to another, monitoring traffic in and out of the variety store. Sometimes she napped in the middle of Route 30. . . . She belonged to everyone and no one.

JON KATZ

SNOW DAY

Noticed it on a snowy day? The grown-ups are all going about with long faces, but look at the children—and the dogs? They know what snow's made for.

C. S. LEWIS

NOTES